Mexico

CULTURES AND CELEBRATIONS

Greg Banks

PICTURE CREDITS

Cover: Feast Day fireworks at San Miguel de Allende, Mexico © Danny Lehman/Corbis/Tranz.

page 1 © Macduff Everton/Corbis/Tranz; page 4 (bottom left) © Morton Beebe/Corbis/Tranz; page 4 (bottom right) © Hans Georg Roth/Corbis/Tranz; page 5 (top) © Larry Dale Gordon/Image Bank/Getty Images; page 5 (bottom left) © Michael S. Yamashita/Corbis/Tranz; page 5 (bottom right) © Richard T. Nowitz/Corbis/Tranz; page 6 © Bettmann/Corbis/Tranz; page 8 © Douglas Peebles/Corbis/Tranz; page 9 (left) © Robert Holmes/Corbis/Tranz; page 9 (top right), Artville; page 9 (bottom right) © Bill Bettencourt/Foodpix/Getty Images; page 10 © Chuck Savage/Corbis/Tranz; page 11 © Daniel Aguilar/Reuters/Stock Image Group; page 12 (top) © Burstein Collection/Corbis/Tranz; page 12 (bottom) © The Granger Collection, New York; page 13 © Sergio Dorantes/Corbis/Tranz; page 14 © Charles & Josette Lenars/Corbis/Tranz; page 15 (top) © David H. Wells/Corbis/Tranz; page 15 (bottom)© Stephanie Maze/Corbis/Tranz; page 16 (top) © Morton Beebe/Corbis/Tranz; page 16 (bottom) © Tim De Waele/Corbis/Tranz; page 21 © Danny Lehman/Corbis/Tranz; page 22 © Lawrence Migdale/Stone/Getty Images; page 23 (top) © Tom Owen Edmunds/Image Bank/Getty Images; page 23 (bottom) © David Hiser/Stone/Getty Images; page 24 (top) © Lindsay Hebberd/Corbis/Tranz; page 24 (bottom) © David Hiser/Stone/Getty Images; page 25 (top), Photodisc; page 25 (bottom) © Michael Townsend/Stone/Getty Images; page 26 © David Hiser/Stone/Getty Images; page 29 (top), Photodisc; page 29 (bottom), Digital Vision.

Produced through the worldwide resources of the National Geographic Society, John M. Fahey, Jr., President and Chief Executive Officer; Gilbert M. Grosvenor, Chairman of the Board; Nina D. Hoffman, Executive Vice President and President, Books and Education Publishing Group.

PREPARED BY NATIONAL GEOGRAPHIC SCHOOL PUBLISHING
Ericka Markman, Senior Vice President and President, Children's Books and Education Publishing Group; Steve Mico, Vice President and Editorial Director; Marianne Hiland, Executive Editor; Richard Easby, Editorial Manager; Jim Hiscott, Design Manager; Kristin Hanneman, Illustrations Manager; Matt Wascavage, Manager of Publishing Services; Sean Philpotts, Production Manager.

EDITORIAL MANAGEMENT
Morrison BookWorks, LLC

PROGRAM CONSULTANTS
Dr. Shirley V. Dickson, Program Director, Literacy, Education Commission of the States; Margit E. McGuire, Ph.D., Professor of Teacher Education and Social Studies, Seattle University.

CONTENT REVIEWER
Alejandro Negrin, Director, Mexican Cultural Institute, Washington, D.C.

National Geographic Theme Sets program developed by Macmillan Science and Education Australia Pty Limited.

Published by the National Geographic Society
1145 17th Street, N.W.
Washington, D.C. 20036-4688

ISBN: 978-0-7922-4766-1
ISBN: 0-7922-4766-3

Printed in China by The Central Printing (Hong Kong) Ltd.
Quarry Bay, Hong Kong
Supplier Code: OCP May 2018
Macmillan Job: 804263
Cengage US PO: 15308030

MEA10_May18_S

Contents

Cultures and Celebrations

Culture is the way people in one group live that makes them different from other groups. Culture is made up of many different things. These include traditions, language, dress, ceremonies, and other ways of life that a group of people share. Celebrations are also an important part of culture. By looking at countries such as Mexico, Italy, Japan, and Egypt, you can see how cultural practices bring people together.

Key Concepts ....

1. Every society has a way of life that people share. This way of life makes up its culture.

2. Culture and celebrations help create a sense of national identity among people.

3. Some parts of culture change, but modern and traditional activities can exist side by side.

Four Different Cultures

Mexico

Mexican culture includes Spanish and Mexican Indian customs.

Italy

Regional customs and the Roman Catholic religion are important in Italian culture.

In this book you will learn about the customs and celebrations that make up the culture of Mexico.

Japan

Modern city life and ancient customs and values combine in the culture of Japan.

Egypt

The Islamic religion and a strong sense of history are important in Egypt's culture.

The Culture of Mexico

Step into Mexico. What do you see? You see people that are a mix of Spanish and Mexican Indian. You may see children playing soccer or marbles. Listen to the children speak. You hear mostly Spanish, but also Mexican Indian languages. Can you see churches? Most Mexicans are Roman Catholic, but some follow other religions. Look and listen. What else can you see and hear?

People have lived in Mexico for a very long time. Mexican Indians were the first people in Mexico. Then Spanish people came in the 1500s. For many years, Mexico was ruled by Spain.

Hernan Cortes, seated, led Spanish soldiers into Mexico in 1519.

Mexico Today

Mexico is a country in North America. Its people have a way of life that mixes the past with the present. Some parts of this way of life come from Mexican Indian groups. Some parts of this way of life come from the Spanish.

Look at the map below. It shows you where Mexico is located.

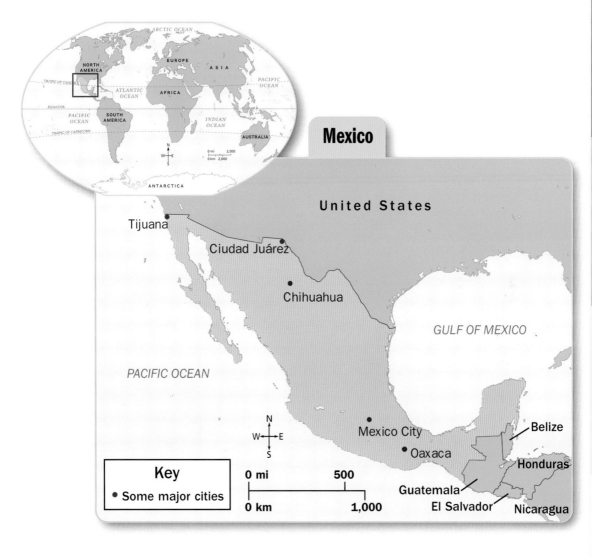

Key Concept 1 Every society has a way of life that people share. This way of life makes up its culture.

Societies and Their Cultures

Every **society** has its own way of life, or culture. Some parts of culture are easy to see. You can see how people dress and what they eat. Others are not so easy to see. You cannot see what people believe. You cannot always see what their **values** are.

> culture
> the language, dress, values, celebrations, and other ways of life that a group of people share

These girls are dressed in traditional Mexican dancing costumes.

Mexican Food

Have you ever eaten a **tortilla**? A tortilla (tore-*tee*-yuh) is a flat bread made of corn meal or wheat flour. Tortillas are a food that is part of Mexican culture.

Frijoles (free-*hoh*-les), or beans, are another important food in Mexico. Frijoles can be eaten with tortillas or alone. Mexicans often add spices to frijoles.

Chilies are an important flavor in Mexican food.

Meat and vegetables can be wrapped in a wheat-flour tortilla to make a *taco*.

This woman is cooking tortillas made of corn meal.

Mexican Values

Spending time with family and friends is important to Mexicans. This is one of their values. Mexican people like to invite guests to their homes. It is a sign of friendship. Mexicans like to say, *"Mi casa es tu casa."* This means, "My house is your house."

Family and friends enjoy celebrating special occasions together.

Culture and National Identity

Certain things bring the people of Mexico together. One of these things is the Mexican flag. Other things are Mexican art and language. **Celebrations** also bring Mexicans together. These things give the people a national identity.

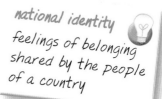

national identity
feelings of belonging shared by the people of a country

Flag

The colors of the Mexican flag stand for values that are important to Mexicans. The green stripe stands for hope and victory. It reminds Mexicans of their fight with Spain to be a free country. The white stripe stands for the purity of Mexico's values. The red stripe stands for the bravery of Mexico's national heroes.

Soccer fans wave the flag after a victory for the national team.

Art

Mexico's art is an important part of its culture. People in Mexico have made pottery for thousands of years. They often paint their pottery with bright patterns.

A Mayan plate made in Mexico more than 1,000 years ago

Do you know what a **mural** is? A mural is a large painting on a wall. One of Mexico's most famous artists was Diego Rivera. He lived from 1886 to 1957. Rivera painted murals about Mexican life. His wife, Frida Kahlo, was also a well-known Mexican painter.

Mexican artist Diego Rivera painted this mural in Mexico City.

Frida Kahlo painted this portrait of herself in the 1930s.

Music

Music is important in Mexican culture. Have you ever heard a *mariachi* band? Mariachis are men who sing. They also play guitars, trumpets, and violins. Mariachis often wear frilly shirts and hats called *sombreros* when they play. Mariachi bands are a colorful part of Mexican culture.

Language

Spanish is the official language of Mexico. Most Mexicans speak Spanish every day. However, many Mexicans speak Mexican Indian languages as well as Spanish. These languages are all part of Mexico's culture and national identity.

A mariachi band plays for dancers in a park.

Celebrations

Mexican people have many national celebrations that stand for their values. One of these is the Day of the Dead. On this day, Mexicans remember their **ancestors** and other relatives who have died. Often, the Mexican people build altars for this celebration. An altar is a platform on which food, flowers, and other objects are placed. Then family members gather together to honor their dead ancestors.

Cinco de Mayo is a celebration about Mexican history. Cinco de Mayo celebrates a Mexican victory over the French in 1862. Today, people celebrate Cinco de Mayo with parades and fireworks. They sometimes wear costumes and act out the Mexican victory.

Toy skeletons made for the Day of the Dead

Changing Culture

Over time, cultures may change. Modern ways or practices come into a culture. These new ways often replace the old, or **traditional**, ways. But sometimes, modern and traditional ways exist side by side.

traditional
handed down
through time

Dress

In small villages and on farms, Mexican people wear simple clothes that suit the weather. These styles of dress have not changed much in hundreds of years.

Businessmen in modern dress

Mexicans living in cities dress much like people do in the United States. For special celebrations, some Mexicans wear traditional costumes. A woman might wear an embroidered blouse, a sash, and a skirt decorated with ribbons or beads. Sometimes, Mexican people wear traditional masks to celebrations.

Girls in traditional costumes

Games

Sports have always been an important part of Mexican culture. A Mexican Indian group called the Aztecs played a game like soccer. The players had to get a round ball through a stone ring. They could not use their hands. But they could use their knees, hips, and thighs. Many courts where Aztecs played this game still exist.

Aztecs used to play a game on courts like this one.

Today, soccer is very popular in Mexico. Many Mexican people play soccer with their friends. They also like to watch professional teams play in Mexico. Many people in Mexico support the Mexican national team.

Soccer is the most popular sport in Mexico. Fans watch the national team play against teams from all over the world.

Think About the **Key Concepts**

Think about what you read. Think about the photographs and illustrations. Use these to answer the questions. Share what you think with others.

1. Name at least two values that are part of the culture of the people in this book.

2. How have the flag, art, and language helped give these people a national identity?

3. Tell about two cultural celebrations in this country.

4. Discuss at least two examples of how modern parts of culture and traditional parts of culture exist side by side.

Comparison Chart

A chart allows you to find specific facts quickly and easily. You can learn new ideas without having to read many words. Charts use words and a box-like layout to present ideas.

There are different kinds of charts. This chart of countries and their cultures is a **comparison chart**. It compares information about different countries.

How to Read a Comparison Chart

1. Read the title.
The title tells you the subject, or what the chart is about.

2. Read the column headings.
Columns go from top to bottom. The heading at the top of each column tells you what kind of information is in the column.

3. Read the row headings.
Rows go from side to side. The headings in the left column name the countries you will get information about as you read across the rows.

4. Connect the information as you read.
Read across each row to find information about a subject. Read down each column to compare information.

Countries and Their Cultures

Country	Population	Land Area Square kilometers	Capital City	Main Religion	Flag
Mexico	104,959,594	1,923,040	Mexico City	Roman Catholicism	
Italy	58,057,477	294,020	Rome	Roman Catholicism	
Japan	127,333,002	374,744	Tokyo	Shinto and Buddhism	
Egypt	76,117,421	995,450	Cairo	Islam	

What Are the Facts?

Write sentences telling all the facts you learned about one of the countries in the chart. Share with a classmate who chose a different country. What is similar about the countries? What is different?

Photo Essay

A **photo essay** is a group of photographs and captions that tell about an event or place.

Photo essays are usually printed in magazines or newspapers. Their purpose is to show images connected to the event or place that they are about. Photo essays also try to help people understand the feelings or emotions behind the event or place.

Dia de los Muertos
A Mexican Celebration

Celebrations are an important part of Mexican culture. National holidays, like *Dia de los Muertos*, the Day of the Dead, help people share their culture. This holiday began with the ancient Aztecs. They believed that the spirits of their dead ancestors could return to visit them. When the Spanish took over Mexico, they kept the festival. They added some new parts to it.

Day of the Dead celebrations are held every year on November 1 and 2. People remember family members who have died. It is a happy celebration. These women are placing flowers on a family member's grave.

The **title** tells the topic of the photo essay.

The **introduction** gives an overview of the topic.

Captions add information and help explain the pictures.

Photographs tell the story of the topic in pictures.

Some Mexican families make altars and lay out *ofrendas*, or offerings, for the Day of the Dead. They decorate the altars with flowers, food, and sometimes a few of the possessions of their relatives who have died.

Mexican children make trinkets for the ofrendas. They also join in a special family meal. During these celebrations, older family members teach young people the history of their family and their community.

These skulls are made of candy to celebrate the Day of the Dead. Each is given the name of an ancestor.

On the Day of the Dead, families and friends walk through the streets. They walk with special skeletons they have made. The smiling skeleton toys help the people to enjoy thinking of their dead relatives. The skeletons are funny, not spooky. People also carry flowers to the cemetery.

Many Mexicans visit cemeteries on the Day of the Dead. They may ask a mariachi band to play and sing. The band helps them celebrate.

This woman has brought a photo of a relative to the cemetery. She has also brought flowers. In this way, she celebrates the life of her loved one who has died.

People often take flowers to the cemetery. They stay at the cemetery all night beside the graves of their loved ones.

Whole cemeteries may be lit up at night on the Day of the Dead. This is because so many people bring lights and candles to the graves.

The Day of the Dead is an important celebration throughout Mexico. Family members come together to prepare for the day and take part in the celebration. It is an important part of their culture.

Apply the Key Concepts

Key Concept 1 Every society has a way of life that people share. This way of life makes up its culture.

Activity Make a chart with two columns. Think about your American culture or the culture of your heritage. In the first column, list some parts of your culture that are easy to see. In the second column, list some parts of your culture that are not easy to see.

Easy to See	Hard to See
dress	

Key Concept 2 Culture and celebrations help create a sense of national identity among people.

Activity Draw a picture of the Mexican flag and a picture of the American flag. Write a caption under each flag explaining what the colors and symbols of the flags mean. You may need to do some research about the American flag. Then write about the similarities and differences between the American and Mexican flags.

The flag symbolizes . . .

Key Concept 3 Some parts of culture change, but modern and traditional activities can exist side by side.

Activity List some traditional parts of Mexican culture. Next to each one, write whether it is still practiced today. Describe any modern practices that exist alongside it or have replaced it.

1. Making pottery	1. Still practiced

Create Your Own Photo Essay

Mexico's culture includes many practices, traditions, and celebrations. You have read about some of them. Now it's time to think about your culture. Get ready to make your own photo essay about your culture. You may choose your American culture or the culture of your heritage.

1. Study the Model

Look back at the photo essay on pages 21–26. Think about how the photos and captions work together to tell a story. How do the photos show the actions and feelings of the people? How do the captions help you understand the photos? You'll want to think about these things as you plan your own essay.

Creating a Photo Essay

◆ Write a title that tells the topic of the photo essay.

◆ Choose photographs that show different things about the topic.

◆ Organize the photographs into a story.

◆ Write an introduction that summarizes the topic.

◆ Write captions that help tell the story.

2. Choose and Plan Your Topic

Look through books and websites for photos that show your culture. The topic of your photo essay should be an event, place, or group of people in your culture. Try to find several different photos that relate to one event, place, or group of people. Make sure that you can find enough photos related to the topic. Then read about your topic. Make notes on what you find.

3. Organize Your Materials

Photocopy photos you want to use from books and magazines, or print photos from the Internet. Look for photos that show people and their actions. Choose the photos that tell your story best. Your photos should cover different parts of your topic, and some should show people's feelings. Write down facts about each photo. You can use these to write captions.

Many Americans have picnics on the Fourth of July.

4. Make a Draft

Think about the best order for the photos in your photo essay. Which one introduces the topic best? Lay out the photos in an order that makes them easy to understand. Write one caption for each photo. The captions should help tell the story. Then write an introduction. The introduction should summarize the topic and get people interested in your photo essay.

5. Revise and Edit

Look at the photos and read your text. Correct any mistakes. Do the photos tell a story? Do the captions and introduction add information and help explain the photos? Paste the photos onto sheets of paper in the order you've chosen. Put your title and introduction on a separate page. Copy your captions carefully under each photo.

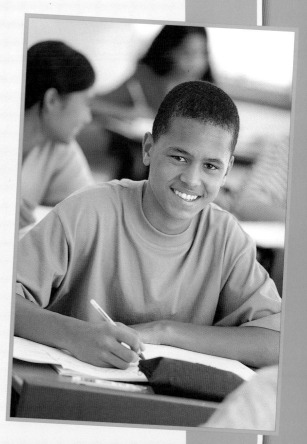

Create Your Own Photo Exhibition

Now you can share your work. An exhibition is a display that you might see in a gallery or a museum. Follow the steps below to make a photo exhibition.

How to Make a Photo Exhibition

1. Make each photo essay into a poster.
Paste the pages of the photo essay on poster board.

2. Decide on an arrangement for the photo essays.
You might want to group essays with similar subjects. For example, photo essays about celebrations could go on one wall.

3. Display the photo essays.
Make sure they are at a good height. People should be able to look at the photos without looking too far up or down.

4. Choose a name for the exhibition.
The name should describe the theme of the exhibition.

5. Make a catalogue for the exhibition.
A catalogue tells visitors to an exhibition about the items on display. Write a description for each photo essay. Label the descriptions with the titles of the photo essays, and type them in the order in which they have been arranged on the walls. Make copies for the people who will visit the exhibition.

6. Have a grand opening for your exhibition.
You could invite parents or students from another class. Give each guest a catalogue, and let them look at the exhibition.

Glossary

ancestors – family members who lived years ago

celebrations – special activities done to show that a holiday or other event is important to a group of people

culture – the language, dress, values, celebrations, and other ways of life that a group of people share

mural – a large painting done on a wall

national identity – feelings of belonging shared by the people of a country

society – a group of people who live together in the same community or country

tortilla – a flat bread made of corn meal or wheat flour that is a traditional food in Mexico

traditional – handed down through time

values – the beliefs and standards that are important to a person or a group of people

Index